I HAVE A
TESTIMONY

ONE MAN'S ACCOUNT OF
MODERN DAY MIRACLES

BRAD SMITH

Dedication

This book is dedicated to my best friend, confidant, and wife of 19 years, Blonnie -- You are my pride and joy. Your never-ending love and support mean the world to me. There's no other person on the face of this Earth I'd rather be married to.

To my boys, Aaron and Adam -- I am so proud to be your father. I pray that this compilation of events causes you to look back and realize just how much the Holy Spirit was involved in our lives. My desire is for you to go much further with God than I ever have, so that one day, your faith will be passed down to your own children.

To my late mother in-law, Sandra Lee Holland -- You remind me that the greatest miracle one can receive is not the healing of the body, but the gift of eternal life. You ran your race with grace. Rest in Jesus. We will see you soon.

Acknowledgments

First and foremost, I am thankful for Jesus Christ. Not only did He save me from sin, but He also trusted me enough to put me in His ministry. I will do my best to never let Him down.

I'm so grateful for my mom, Pennie Shocklee. She has always believed in me no matter what I've decided to do with my life. With this type of support, a man can do anything he puts his mind to.

I owe a special thanks to my spiritual father, Shane Warren, who has challenged to not be satisfied with the mundane. His example has caused a generation to love Jesus and chase the supernatural. I want to be just like him when I grow up.

I Have A Testimony

One Man's Account Of Modern Day Miracles by
Brad Smith

Published by Brad Smith Ministries

Printed by Kindle Direct Publishing

Printed in the United States.

ISBN-13 (Paperback): 9798687671750

Forward

Mikey Cheshier

Once again, the bush of Kenya was our destination. Our goal as always was to reach lost souls for Christ. These trips are seasoned with challenges, and the overshadowing possibility of the unknown makes for an exciting time of exploration.

It had become a tradition when traveling with Brad to ask him, "What are you believing for this time?" He responded, "I believe that a blind person will receive their sight." He added, "Come on, somebody! (With a stammer, a shout, and a trembling voice)" I joined with him in the expectation that we would see God move in power. I must confess: That is exactly what happened! Later on our trip, a blind woman received her sight. Glory to our Lord!

Miracles - They've been cornerstone proofs of the Divine since the beginning of human history. For some reason beyond clear understanding, it's become less fashionable to talk about them in today's church culture.

I'm so excited that Brad has been moved upon by the Holy Spirit to share stories and experiences that will inspire the generations to come to believe for even greater things. In order to see how essential miracles are to the faith we possess, we should would look to the words of the worker of miracles — Jesus, the Son of God. Consider, when the apostle Peter was called upon to make an account of Jesus, he said, "Jesus of Nazareth, a man approved of God among you by miracles wonders and signs" (Acts 2:22 KJV). Then again, Jesus Himself said, "Though you believe not me, believe the works" (John 10:38 KJV). Consider also when John the baptizer sent disciples to see if Jesus was the Christ or if they should seek another, Jesus said, "Go your way, and tell John what things ye have seen and heard; how that the blind see, the lame walk, and the lepers are cleansed" (Luke 7:22 KJV).

Testimonies encourage the believer to trust Jesus for the impossible. We as people often need reminded that it's ok to have audacious faith. We are to utter the type of prayers that make our flesh (and others) nervous. This is the kind of faith that pleases God!

This subject or miracles is so personally precious to me. As a child, I was severly burned. Then, later in life, I was invaded by terminal cancer, struck by vehicles, contracted malaria, and dodged death more times than I can count. I'm fully aware that I'm breathing borrowed air!

Through the years, Brad has shared his personal stories with me. I've watched him trust God through the difficulties of life. I'm persuaded that his perspective on faith and his personal experiences position him to be a voice for God to this generation. I pray that you will not only be blessed by the testimonies enclosed, but that you become inspired to believe

God for yourself. He specialized in difficult situations. Nothing is impossible to Him!

About The Author

Brad Smith's passion is defined in one word— Souls. At age 13, he accepted Jesus as his Savior and was filled with the Holy Spirit. At age 14, he had a dream of lost people screaming out in Hell. Awakened in a cold sweat, he heard a voice telling him to preach the Gospel of Jesus Christ.

That call has led him on a lifetime of adventures. From the local church, the prison system, and Africa's darkest corners, he has endeavored to spend his life on the Great Commission.

Brad and his wife Blonnie have pastored several turnaround churches, watching life return to barren places. Aside from his first love of the local church, he has also invested in missionary evangelism and church planting.

In 2019, he founded Brad Smith Ministries, a nonprofit organization that was established to do missionary work and train leaders. In 2020, Brad Smith Ministries partnered with the Kenyan Assemblies of God and Mikey and Shereen Cheshier Ministries to establish Kilimanjaro School of Missions, a training center raising up Kenyan missionaries to reach the surrounding nations of Africa.

Brad and Blonnie are both credentialed ministers with the Assemblies of God. Together with their two children, they reside in northwest Oklahoma.

TABLE OF CONTENTS

Introduction

Have you ever been fascinated by the supernatural? I have. Growing up, I read books by all of my spiritual heroes: Smith Wigglesworth, A.A. Allen, Oral Roberts, Kathryn Kuhlman, and others. I'd read intently and think about how marvelous it would be to see such miracles in my day! First of all, I don't mean to insinuate that I never saw the hand of God at work.. To be clear, salvation and Spirit baptism are both supernatural events. However, I didn't see the type of power displays recorded in the writings of the New Testament.

I was raised in a Pentecostal church. Pentecostals believe that the nine gifts of the Holy Spirit are still in operation today. All throughout school, I was made fun of because I went to "that" church. By "that" church, I mean the type of church that speaks in tongues and handles snakes. Well, the snakes part isn't true!

On any given Sunday, we would worship our hearts out. Music is a huge part of our culture. Whether they were hymns or "chorus" songs, we would sing them, sing them again, and sing them some more! Exuberant praise is to be expected in our services. We're known for being loud. You know, we're the type of people who say "Amen," "Glory," or "Hallelujah" when the Spirit hits us just right!

In a Spirit-filled church service, there are times when it gets oddly quiet. When this happens, a person will often feel moved upon by God to speak out in tongues. They will stand up and loudly lift their voice. This is known as a "message in tongues." After the message was given, someone else would stand up and interpret what they felt like the Holy Spirit was saying. Did I forget to mention that this interpretation was often made in King James English? Then, a powerful time of prayer and response would happen around the altars. Maybe the pastor would preach his sermon afterward -- maybe he wouldn't. We called these type of meetings, "run away" services.

Though it may seem like I'm poking fun a little, I promise you this: I wouldn't trade those experiences for anything. It was moments just like these that intensified my appetite to experience God's power. Even though I had sensed the presence of God in undeniable ways, I can't recall ever seeing miracles of a Biblical caliber.

What type of miracles am referring I to? I'm talking about the type where tumors fall off of people, cancerous growths disappear, blind eyes pop open, deaf ears are unstopped, and the demon possessed are delivered and set free by the power of Jesus' name.

Not seeing these type of exploits on a personal level set me on a journey to experience them for myself. But why? So I could feel good about myself? So I could have a big name in

Christendom or a vast platform for ministry? No! There's only one simple reason: That's how it's supposed to be! According to Mark 16:16, "These signs shall follow them that believe..." A Gospel with no power is no Gospel at all!

Before you dive into the accounts enclosed in the chapters to come, I assure you that these events transpired exactly as stated. Where it's appropriate, names and locations have been used for validity and context. I have nothing to gain by falsifying information, exaggerating numbers, or by stretching the truth. My one desire is for you to read these testimonies with hopes that the same faith will awaken in your own heart.

Buckle your seatbelt, hold on, and enjoy the ride. You're about to see firsthand how God can show up and show out in the lives of His children.

"There are two ways you can live: You can live as if nothing is a miracle or live as if everything is a miracle."

-Albert Einstein

CHAPTER ONE

"Preach
My Gospel"

M y faith journey is one that's been filled with great
excitement. There's not been one boring moment.
First of all, I'd like to say how grateful I am to have grown
up in a Christian home. Unfortunately, everyone hasn't had
this privilege. For the most part, my family made sure that I
was raised in the faith. Sunday School, summer camps, and
late night revivals were the normal way of life. I wouldn't trade
anything for my spiritual foundation.

I was raised in an extremely small Arkansas town. I was
blessed to have some great friends. One particular family that
lived next door had three boys. Of those three, Kelston and I
became best friends. On occassion, I'd go to church with his
family. We were practically inseperable. We'd sit in the backyard

after school and discuss the stories of the Bible and dream about doing great things for God.

In the seventh grade, we had a nice woman who taught the gifted and talented program. She was a fun-loving, eccentric lady! Her magnetic personality really caused the students to flock to her. We later found out that she was a devout believer! Aside from teaching, she was enrolled in an extension Bible college through her church. In today's politically correct culture, this would've caused an uproar, but she invited a group of us students to church.

It was at Magnolia Christian Center in Magnolia, Arkansas that I met some of the most radical believers that I'd ever encountered. I didn't see this passion at any other church I'd visited. Randy Goudeau, the youth pastor, was wild and crazy for Christ. He'd come to the high school at lunch, stand up on a table, and preach until students got saved. When Pastor Randy would find out where they were hanging out on the weekends, he would show up and preach from the back end of a truck!

Some might think this was an ineffective mode of outreach, but in rural America, we had a fast-growing youth ministry of over 120 students. When I saw the fire, zeal, and passion of those believers, I knew I wanted what they had. I had grown up in a Spirit-filled church, but I'd never received the baptism of the Spirit myself. I needed this experience -- and I needed it right now.

One night at youth, Pastor Randy preached a powerful message on the need for the Holy Spirit. He often preached on living holy, stressing how this was impossible to do without God's help. After giving the invitation, teenagers began to pack the altar until literally, there was no more room. Adult volunteers hurried to move the stackable chairs just to accommodate the flood of hungry souls.

He encouraged people to lift their hands to Heaven. Biblically speaking, the lifting of hands is accompanied with prayer and worship and is understood as an outward sign of surrender. As people began to cry out to God in prayer, he began to lay hands on them. As he did, they began to speak with tongues. When he prayed for me, I felt something. It was like a surge of raw electricity went from the top of my head and out of my toes!

I didn't speak with tongues at this exact moment. There's a reason for that, which I may explain later, but I knew that I didn't fully receive what I'd come for. I wasn't satisfied. The next day, I began to pray and talk to God about what I'd experienced. Of all places, I was in the shower getting ready for school. Before I realized what had happened, I lost my English and began to speak in the most fluent, beautiful language. At that moment, I was filled with the Holy Spirit.

This experience we refer to as "Spirit baptism" changed my life forever. As a teenager, I got involved in a local church, began to play drums on a worship team, and helped lead a small group. I boldly shared my faith with my classmates, teachers, and family. I was unashamed.

That season of life was the best of times and the worst of times. My parents ended up divorcing. To overstate the obvious, this caused a lot of family hurt. As a teenager, I was stuck in a bad situation: I was forced to choose which parent I wanted to live with. No pressure, right? My dad kept the house while mom moved to the next town over and started a new life.

Wanting to be a piece of stability in her otherwise unsecure world, I moved in with mom. Because she was getting back on her feet, finances were very slim. For a very short season, we ended up renting two bedrooms from a lady that worked at her job. It wasn't an ideal situation, but for the time being, it sufficed. It was in the back bedroom of that double-wide mobile home that my destiny was altered forever — I had a dream.

First of all, I'm not a dreamer. I know people who seem to have them on a consistent basis. Some of them are spiritual in nature -- Others just seem like bad indigestion! Not me! I can only recall a few in the entirety of my life. For whatever reason, this isn't the way the Holy Spirit chooses to speak to me. Usually, He speaks to me through an inner impression, a vision, or through the Scriptures. Since this dream was so vivid, I knew I needed to pay attention. It was not normal.

In this dream, which is way too extensive to explain in a few chapters, God showed me my life. Through an illustration of grapes, a vineyard, and a pruning vinedresser, He showed me what it's genuinely like to be connected to Him. Hooked up to Christ, we are fruitful and prosperous. The very life that flows in us comes straight from Him. All of the fruit a branch produces is a direct result of the vine it's connected to. Although I never saw God's face or form, His voice was embodying. It was as if He was literally standing over my shoulder narrating the whole thing.

Then, the scene changed. As fast as a blink of an eye, I began to fall. The best I can explain it to you is like this: It was as if I'd experienced a free falling elevator ride from the top story of a massive skyscraper. I could feel the heat, sense the desperation., and hear the screaming and wailing of lost humanity. It was the worst sound the human eardrum could ever hear.

As I began to fall faster and faster, the darkness enveloped all around me. People screamed for relief, but their cries were unanswered. Though it was dark, the fire raged. Words aren't adequate, but it was the most hopeless feeling I'd ever felt. Jesus was showing me at that moment just what my life would be like connected to His purpose-- Fruitful, prosperous, and alive. In the same breath, He showed me what it's like for people who ultimately reject His goodness. I can tell you this: Hell is no joke. Eternity is way too long to be wrong!

Have you ever fallen asleep only to wake up suddenly, feeling as if you were falling? It's accompanied with the jarring sensation of "catching yourself." That's what happened to me! Awakened, I abruptly sat up in the bed. I attempted to catch my breath while processing what had happened. My heart was hammering out of my chest and my bed was soaked with sweat. I immediately heard an audible voice that said, "Preach My Gospel." It was so loud that I literally thought that God Himself was physically manifested in the room!

Sadly, the subject of Hell is absent in most sermons today. This is a tragic reality. Why? The only way men can stay out of this wicked place is if they accept Jesus as Lord. Someone has to tell them! The wages of sin is death, and payday is coming very soon! If people die without Christ, their judgement is eternal fire for all of eternity. This is why I'm so passionate about evangelism. We must tell people that Jesus still saves!

I once heard it said that there are two significant days in a person's life: The day he is born and the day he finds out why. This day, I discovered my purpose -- To preach His Gospel. There are many things in life I've doubted. From time to time, I've wondered if I might've missed God on a few life decisions. I've pondered if I should have stayed some place instead of leaving, or left some place instead of staying. Yet, in all of life's hardships, I've never doubted His calling.

"Every miracle in the Bible first started as a problem."

*- **Author Unknown***

CHAPTER TWO
"Baptized With Fire"

This particular miracle is one that I'll never forget. It's forever etched into my mind. In 2015, we took a rather large team into the deep bush of Kenya to hunt for lost souls. For those of you who want to know what "the bush" is, it's the unpopulated, grassy areas of Africa that lack roads, utilities, and other modern luxuries of the western hemisphere. In other words, the bush is when you drive until the road stops -- and then you keep going!

I have developed a deep love for the Masai people. Their dress is very colorful, representing their patterns and cultural differences, distinguishing between the other regional tribes. The children are incredibly pleasant to interact with. One may think that because they lack the things most of us take for granted, they must be miserable. After all, what American child do you know that can survive without an iPad, video games, and name brand shoes? These kids might be poor, but they don't seem to know it! A Kenyan boy or girl's bright smile can light up a room and warm the coldest of hearts. After no more than five or ten minutes in their presence, you begin to contemplate how you might take them back home with you.

On this particular trip, our group had split in two and went in opposite directions. It's always a blessing when we can do that because it means that our fruit can be multiplied. By going from village to village, we led over 1,000 people to Christ in a few short days. I don't know about you, but we call that successful ministry! One thing that marked this mission as unique was that we ended up visiting several primary schools. That was surprising to me being that we were in an unreached territory.

When I use the term "unreached," in relation to foreign missions, what I mean is that a particular group of people has had little or no exposure at all to the message of Jesus.

Even though this region was unreached by religious influence, it was obvious that some with a passion for education had beat us to them. I could stop and preach right there, but for now, I'll move on. It's likely they founded the school and left it in the hands of the locals. Children's ministry is particularly new in Kenya. Up until about ten years ago or so, it was nonexistent. Children were to be seen and not heard, and they weren't included in church attendance numbers. It's as if they weren't even considered to be people. It's sad to miss out on such a valuable harvest!

When we drove up to the school, perhaps their first thought upon seeing a van carrying white-skinned people is that we were coming to teach English. They ran out and gladly met us with smiles as big as the state of Texas. The Masai are very hospitable people.

To those of us who don't speak a foreign language, communication can be a significant barrier. Most of these kids learn some pieces of English in school, but it's not their primary language. To get over this hurdle of communication, we take skilled translators with us. On this particular day, a pastor from the Assemblies of God church accompanied us. When everyone gathered around us to see what was going on, Bishop Sayo asked the school headmistress for permission to address the students. Of course, this was fine because they rarely pass up the opportunity to speak to a visitor. After all, how often do they get to see white people?

As the headmistress called for an assembly, approximately 120 children, grades 1- 5, gathered together to see what we we might share. Would it be suckers? Clothing? Literature? While we did have candy, what they didn't realize is that they were about to experience the Bread of Life! These boys and girls were about to experience church for the very first time. Meagan Barbier, a young minister from South Louisiana, along with her husband Kody, accompanied us on this mission. She had never "preached" before, and was presented the opportunity to share Jesus with these kids. She was very nervous! At the end of her first message, along with a great translator's help, all of those boys and girls came forward to accept Jesus as Lord! It was an amazing sight to behold!

Bishop Sayo, also having a heart for children, encouraged us to pray for them to receive the Holy Spirit. According to Acts 2, when the Holy Spirit came down upon the early believers, they all began to speak in other tongues. John went a little further in Luke 3:16 when he said, "….He shall baptize you with the Holy Spirit and with fire."

This was the most pure, genuine experience I'd ever seen before. Grady Watson, an evangelist friend from Arkansas, was also present with me. Together we were praying quietly to ourselves, earnestly anticipating what the Holy Spirit would do in the moments to come. We were on edge!

Lions are known as fierce predators in the African bush. The mention of them carries a sense of reverence and fear. Proverbs 21:8 says, "The wicked flee when no one pursues them, but the righteous are bold as a lion." These children would need boldness that only the Holy Spirit can give as they live out their newfound faith in the countryside where His name is scarcely mentioned.

Bishop Sayo asked the kids, "Do you want to be tough like a lion for Jesus?" They replied, "Yes!"

He had them all stand up, and then he asked them to raise their hands to Heaven. He then told them, "I am going to pray for you now." Then, with an authoritative voice, he declared, "One, two, three, receive it now!"

When this happened, one by one, they began to cry. This was followed by uncontrollable shaking. Then, it happened: They all began to speak in other tongues as the Holy Spirit fell upon them. This lasted for quite some time. I'm sure it wasn't as long as it felt like, but in this moment, it was as if time stood still.

As this persisted, many of them could no longer stand up. The glory of God that rested upon them was more than they could bear. They began to fall with nobody touching them. Laying prostrate on the ground, they experienced power for the very first time. They were touched by fire!

The most significant piece of this testimony is the purity of the children's hearts. A skeptic could easily say, "These kids were coerced." or, "They were just mimicking what they had heard." No!

These kids never had access to watch a Benny Hinn crusade, nor had they heard about speaking with tongues. In fact, this was an introductory message to Jesus! With no reference point, that argument is mute. God did this! The same Jesus that poured out His Spirit in Acts 2 touched the children on that day!

"There is nothing impossible with God. All of the impossibility lies within us when we measure God by the limitations of our unbelief."

- Smith Wigglesworth

CHAPTER THREE

"Tongues - A Sign for the Unbeliever"

As you might can tell, I'm passionate about experiencing God's power. I wholeheartedly believe that the Holy Spirit's nine gifts mentioned in 1 Corinthians 11 are still active today. I personally adhere to this not only theologically, but experientially. Church history and modern day accounts all point to the fact that God still moves by unexplainable signs and wonders.

Of all these gifts, perhaps one of the most controversial is what the Bible calls "speaking in tongues." "Tongues," as Paul described it in 1 Corinthians 14:2, is a language that is unknown to the one speaking. It is given by revelation and unlearned through natural means. These languages can be heavenly or Earthly in origin.

In Charismatic circles, we've greatly been criticized by those of more traditional, mainline denominations. They've called us weird, over the top, and in the most extreme cases -- demonic. Without naming names, a prominent minister stated that anyone who speaks in tongues is "demon-possessed!" While others might not make such a hard stance, they would say that we are just emotionally worked up and experiencing a false sense of ecstasy.

I can tell you this: I've found great fulfillment in praying and praising God in other tongues. I believe Romans 8:28 tells us that when we don't know how to pray, the Holy Spirit interceeds both for us and through us. When you couple this fact with 1 Corinthians 14:14 and Jude 20, praying in tongues proves to be a great personal benefit. That being said, prayer isn't the only function of tongues.

According to Paul, 1 Corinthians 14:22 says, "Therefore tongues are for a sign, not to those who believe but to unbelievers; but prophesying is not for unbelievers but for those who believe." This passage shows us that there is indeed another aspect to tongues, which is to be a sign to those who do not believe! This is evident in the very first reference of tongues in Acts. As they were speaking with tongues, Acts 2:11 records, ".....we hear them speaking in our own tongues the wonderful works of God." I'd heard of people experiencing this before, so I began to pray and ask God to let me witness this aspect of tongues myself.

After all, I'd read many accounts of missionaries going into China, Indonesia, or some other country and upon those people receiving the Spirit, they heard them speak in understandable languages other than their natural tongue.

On my first trip into the bush, I was believing to see a blind person healed. It happened. Now, every time I go, I believe God for something different. This time, I had asked Him to allow me to experience tongues as a sign -- not just as a personal prayer language. We always pray for people to receive the baptism of the Spirit, so I went with the expectation of hearing a native praise Christ in fluent English. For that to happen to tribal person would be a miracle. This was my prayer, but God's ways are not always our ways!

Our team had gone out to minister and encountered a woman in distress. She was bent over and writhing in pain. Physically and emotionally traumatized, she was screaming and crying at the top of her lungs.

Her knees had been crushed through a recent accident, resulting in excruciating pain. She needed help in a desperate kind of way! She needed to hear about how Jesus saves, but sometimes it's hard to hear the message through the volume of pain and suffering. This is exactly why compassion ministry, not replacing the Gospel but supplementing it, is useful in accomplishing the mission. There's a reason why Jesus fed the hungry.

Joseph Ntalamia, a great friend and translator, motioned us over to pray. We didn't know the gravity of the whole situation, so we just began to pray the best way we knew how — in other tongues. After all, who knows how to pray better than the Holy Spirit?

As we were praying, I noticed both the woman and Joseph start to look at me in a puzzled fashion. It was if they'd seen a ghost! When I inquired about why they looked startled, Joseph replied, "When you were praying, you were praying fluently in Ke Maa over this woman." Trust me when I say that I was just as shocked as they were. My prayer didn't seem or feel any different. So I asked him, "What did I say?"

Joseph explained to me that in their tribal language, I described in great detail exactly what happened while pleading to God on her behalf. She was not only healed, but she also got saved! God didn't have to do a miracle like this, but perhaps this was needed to soften her heart. After all, no white man from America would ever be able to speak her language. It indeed was a sign to the unbeliever! Once again, God confirmed His Word to us in an unusual way!

"God is not looking for gold vessels or silver vessels. He is looking for willing vessels."

- Kathryn Kuhlman

CHAPTER FOUR
"I See Men like Trees"

I never wanted to go to Kenya. I was satisfied doing what I was doing -- Being a local pastor, supporting missionaries, and living comfortably in my bubble of safety. I've told many people, "I'll never go on a mission's trip." I've learned the hard way to never say what you won't do. At the writing of this book, I've been into Africa nine times and have visited eight different nations.

This miracle happened on my very first trip. Not only was it my first missionary journey, but it was the first major miracle I'd ever witnessed. I'd seen back pain healed, a headache here and there, and other minor ailments allieviated. However, the degree of this miracle was the first of it's kind for me.

At a minster's meeting I was attending, Mikey Cheshier, a young pastor and mission's enthusiast, invited me to come to Kenya to assist in his parents' work. The Cheshier family has served in missionary work for over twenty five years. Our assignment would be to go deep into Kenya's remote region to reach tribal people who had never heard about Jesus. We would take our food, camping supplies, and trek deep into the unknown for eight days, hoping to find lost people.

This type of camping trip is fun, but it's not like the stereotypical camping trip in America. You know, the kind with R.V.'s, bathroom facilities, and barbeque grills. That's not the case at all. Imagine camping in an open, African savannah where you listen to the hyenas laugh, the elephants stomp, and you have the looming awareness that somewhere out there in the dark are the lions.

Warren Camp, a dear family friend, accompanied me into the unknown to look for lost souls. Being my first time out of the country, I didn't know what to expect. I'd never traveled this far from home. I'm so glad Warren came because honestly, I'm not sure anyone back home would have believed my report!

I put out a request to God before we left. I prayed and said, "Jesus, I want to see a blind person healed. I'm tired of just reading about it in books. I want to see this for myself". To some, this may have seemed like a selfish request, but deep down, I knew that God understood the cry of my heart: I was tired of preaching about something I hadn't experienced.

After a day of ministry, we reached another village of potential converts. With the help of our translator, we preached a simplistic Gospel message. When we preached Jesus to them, they received Him with gladness. Many knelt down on the ground, soaking the dust with their tears, asking Jesus to forgive them and to come into their lives.

After every opportunity to receive Christ, we ask them, "Is there anyone sick in your village? We believe the same Jesus who saved you can also heal you." We presented the opportunity to receive healing, but they politely declined. I was never more depressed as a preacher than I was at that moment. How sadistic is it to be upset that no one came forward to receive healing? I didn't want everyone to be well -- I wanted to see a miracle! We started walking back to our vehicle to head to the next village. Before we could make it to the van, we were met with screams.

"Wait!" "Hold up!" "There's an 80-year-old woman who is blind in both eyes. Can you pray for her?" I'd be lying if I told you that my heart wasn't beating violently inside of my chest! My palms got sweaty. My breathing increased. "Sure!", I replied.

As they went back to their little hut to get her, we prayed quietly to ourselves in preparation for what was to come. I could see them walking toward us in the distance. The closer she got, the clearer I could see her face. Her eyes were glazed over, crusted together by dirt, sweat, and infection. She had lost her sight eight years prior. Because she was absent during our salvation presentation, we shared the love of Jesus with her. Upon the hearing of Jesus' sacrifice, She gladly accepted the saving grace of God.

Then, we asked her the obvious question: "Momma, what do you want from God?" To which she replied, "I want to see clearly enough to be able to walk back and forth to the gate of the village and to see my grandchildren again." Because the culture is so different, I didn't want to do anything that might be offensive. I asked our translator to see if it would be ok to lay my hands on her eyes. After a brief discourse in Swahili, she agreed.

As our team came in closer to pray, I laid my hands on her eyes and prayed a bold prayer. I said, "Lord, In the name of Jesus, so that she may know You, I pray for her sight to be restored right now. Blindness, go! Be healed!" As I stepped back, I asked our translator to check and see if there was any change in her vision. She said, "I can see men, but they look like trees."

When she said that, I almost took off running! Had it not been distractive to our purpose, I might would have! This woman had never been to church before. Though she didn't previously know who Jesus was, she quoted a section of Mark 8:24 almost verbatim! It was the passage where Jesus prayed for the blind man a second time. After the first prayer, he also saw "men like trees." Unknown to her, the Holy Spirit allowed this precious lady to use those exact words to verify to us what He was about to do.

What did I do? I prayed again! With excitement, I shouted, "I know how this story ends!' We laid hands on her one more time, and when we did, something unique began to happen.

She began to weep. Her tears were not small and reserved. They were massive.

Instead of clear tears flowing down her cheeks, there were streams of a milky white substance running down her face. In a moment, Jesus eradicted eight years of darkness as the blindness literally melted from her eyes! What we witnessed was Jesus of Nazareth, the same one who walked the streets of Jerusalem, open this woman's sight! As you could imagine, the people were pretty excited about it!

She lifted her hands to Heaven and began to dance and shout. She said, "Praise Jesus" over and over in Swahili. She started walking towards the gate, and while she walked, she took the next few moments describing our clothing colors, facial features, and vehicle description.

That day, Jesus came to restore sight to the blind! Before we even got to the next village, the word of the miracle had beat us there. There was great joy in that region. More people were saved, and a people were changed. Jesus loves the Masai!

"When the Lord spoke into my spirit, 'Expect a miracle,' He said, 'Expect a miracle every day.'"

- Oral Roberts

CHAPTER FIVE
"Tell Him I Can See"

One of my joys in life is investing in the next generation. That's why my wife and I spent many of our early years in youth ministry. While pastoring in Southeast Arkansas, I had the opportunity to take another team to Kenya to do an exploratory mission. If you're wondering what an exploratory mission is, it's where we scout out an unreached area, set up a base camp, and go out in hopes to find lost people.

I had a strong desire to take people from our church with us, but I knew that the pricet of such a trip would be a deterrent. Due to the high cost of international airfare, the total cost of a two week trip can be financially taxing. In order for people to go without money being an issue, I'd need a miracle. I prayed. As a result, the Holy Spirit gave me a creative idea. Our church was located across the street from a hunting store. Each day, deer stands and other outdoor items would be by the road with "For Sale" signs attached to them. It was a redneck paradise! I had a large banner made, a custom deer stand donated, and I launched my plan: I was going "Up In The Air For Kenya." This would involve setting up beside the highway with a sign and rallying the support of the community.

My goal was to stay in this deer stand day and night until I raised every last penny of this money. We received a lot of positive attention as the newspapers, television stations, and local radio got ahold of the story. I don't know exactly how Jesus did it, but He did! Not only did it rain the whole time, but the accompanying winds blew over our volunteer tent!

To make a long story short, God provided. People pledged, and within four days, I raised over $14,000 in cash! Blonnie and I were tasked with praying and selecting two lucky people to accompany us to Kenya. We chose Clarence, one of our board members, and a recent high school graduate named Josh.

I chose Josh because I could see so much potential in him. He was a great guy. Aside from the fact that his family was upstanding in the community, he was one of most popular kids at school. In years prior to this, he was on fire for God. He would speak in the youth group, share his faith at school, and burn bright for Christ. Now, he was struggling.

Despite all of this, the attraction of the world was pulling him. The popularity and attention from the opposite sex caused him to make some unwise decisions. I could totally relate. My own story is very simular. I saw Josh racing towards a path of destruction. I felt that he might benefit from this adventure for many reasons. First of all, I knew he would see the hand of God at work. It would also allow him to experience the hardships of a third world nation. He would soon be going off to a large secular university, and I wanted one last attempt to show him something different. I wanted to make an impact.

With the approval of his parents, Josh joined us. I didn't assign him any specific roles as I did other team members. I simply asked him to pray during our time together and to share an occasional testimony when called upon. As the week progressed, we saw many salvations, healings, and supernatural deliverances. I could tell these things touched him deeply. On the outside, he was a tough guy. Yet, on the inside, he had a compassionate heart. He would weep every single time someone received Jesus.

As we got to our morning assignment, I stepped up to the plate and preached a simple salvation message. Many women, men, and children listened intently, hanging on to every word. Over my shoulder, I could hear some commotion. To be honest, I did my very best to tune it out. I tend to get distracted easily when speaking, and in a place like the bush, you have to be even more aware of your surroundings. After all, the bugs are bigger and the snakes are deadlier than the ones back home. As we got to the end of my message, the noise intensified.

When I turned to look, Josh had his hands laid upon an elderly gentleman. We didn't know it at the time, but he was completely blind in one eye. Josh was praying loud, emotionally charged prayers. His hands were shaking and he was sobbing. The older man just stood there, seemingly unaffected. It was a sight to behold! What I'm about to tell you is hilarious. Had you not been there, you likely wouldn't believe it. First of all, let me clarify: Masai men are tough. They are taught not to show emotion from a very young age. The Masai tribe are not only known for being shepherds, but skilled warriors. To show any type of fear, angst, or outward emotion can be seen as a weakness.

When I turned to address the situation, our translator began to converse with the blind man. All of a sudden, a deep belly laugh came from him. When I asked him what was so funny, he replied, "The man has asked me to please tell the boy to stop crying. He can see now!" As you can imagine, Jesus got everybody's attention in that little village. One by one, young and old, they knelt in the dirt and confessed Jesus as Lord.

A miracle had happened in our midst and we didn't even know it. I'm not certain Josh realized in the moment that he was praying for a blind man. He just felt he needed to pray. This situation taught me two things. First of all, God can use whoever He wills, whenever He wills. Josh was struggling in his faith and God still chose to use him. That will mess with your theology a little! Next, I learned that God's plan for a person's life is forever settled. He never changes His mind.

What a blessing it is to know that when we're obedient, God moves. To top it off, it's not based on what we've done, but on what Jesus did at Calvary! Just as He promised, He confirms the message. We are just the vessels. Be obedient to His leadings and watch to see what He will do. He works through surrendered lives!

"Faith cannot exist where the will of God is unknown."

- F. F. Bosworth

CHAPTER SIX

"I Thought He Was a Beggar"

I've always said that when I write another book, I'm going to call it "Things They Don't Teach You in Bible School." I haven't done it yet, but it's a great topic! When taking most types of theological training, formal or not, there are several "staple" things you learn. You learn about the history of the Bible and how its books were compiled. You're taught about the culture the Bible was written in, which helps you to understand why some things were said and done, and you learn how to interpret the Bible correctly. These things are designed to help you become a better communicator of Biblical truth. After all, that's all a minister does, right?

Wrong answer!

As a youth pastor, I may have believed that. Boy, was I mistaken! I've had to ask the Lord to forgive me so many times for the moments I said, "If I were the pastor, this is what I'd do." If you don't know the intricacies and behind the scenes mechanics of day to day church ministry, you have no idea what you're talking about. As a brand new Lead Pastor, I was pushed head first into a world I wasn't prepared for — Church politics. That would include boards, board meetings, business meetings, annual budgets, and dealing with cranky people.

Sometimes dealing with church leaders, especially those in deep seated positions of authority, can prove to be difficult. Even though you've been brought onboard as the leader, your presence and influence can be perceived as intimidating. In actuality, you become a threat to their influence. I'm convinced that some organizations don't want a leader — They want a whipping boy. They don't want the responsibility of leadership, but they want to be in charge.

I was the new guy. I had followed a long-tenured pastor who had done an amazing job of holding everything steady for over thirty years. Though this was an amazing church with awesome people, the structure of the church revealed a problem. It had deeply entrenched leadership. In our particular denomination, a "church board," or as some might say, a "deacon board" is elected on a rotational term.

A board's legal purpose is to help oversee the operation of an organization. While this is their legal requirement as far as the IRS is concerned, their Biblical role is much different. These individuals are to work with the pastor to fulfill their vision for the church, not work against the pastor to keep their vision for the church! When the latter happens, it's a nightmare.

This board had men on it who had been in their particulae seats for over thirty years. Typically, the rotating board system has term limits. This policy is in place to keep power struggles from developing within the organization.

That wasn't my reality at all. There were no term limits. Popularity and familiarity killed the momentum. I was kept in the dark concerning the church's finances, and nether was I allowed to make any leadership decisions. As a new pastor, I didn't know how to fight or change this faulty system. I struggled through it the best I could. Had I known what I know now, things could've been much different.

Our church was debt-free, and while we didn't have tons of money in the bank, we had well enough to do what we needed to do. God blessed us and the church began to grow. This growth attracted more young people, which required more staff, and eventually led to us needing to upgrade an extremely outdated facility. The power brokers of the church perceived all of the new changes as an infringement on the previous pastor's vision and legacy. I guess they didn't get the memo that he quit!

We needed to renew and refresh many things, but the top need was a media upgrade. Plain and simple, I wanted a single shot video camera to start filming our services and put them online. In a digital age, surely everyone would think this was a good idea, right? Also wrong!

I researched and found the best camera my budget could buy: A small digital camcorder for the extravagant price of $500. I hope you can read my sarcasm. For those with an understanding of camera costs, you know this is about as cheap as it gets! I shot for the lowest budget I could come up with because I wanted to guarantee that they wouldn'tt deny my request. As mentioned before, not being able to make decisions forced me to get approval for even the smallest of things.

At our next board meeting, I compiled all of the information necessary to strike up a deal. My hopes were high that everybody would give a resounding "Yes!" Someone spoke up and said that they didn't think my project was a good idea. They went on to say that we had other physical needs around the church that were more pressing than a camera. That was their way of killing my vision.

After this, we proceeded with the rest of our meeting. Towards the end, another board member mentioned that their grandchild was involved in a sport at a local Christian school. Due to a shortage in private funding, they needed corporate sponsorships for their team to go toward purchasing uniforms.

Churches were offered an advertising opportunity that involved the purchasing of a sign which would display all of the church information It would conveniently be located in a high traffic area of the stadium. Coincidentally, this request was also $500. Surely they would say "No", right? After all, we have "more pressing needs around the church." I was shocked when everybody said "Yes!" I left discouraged and disgruntled Honestly, I was hot!

At the time, our youth pastor was helping me get the media department established. We were brand new to Facebook, Instagram, and other modern modes of communication. He was just as disappointed and frustrated as I was. After all, it's not like we didn't have the money in the bank to do it.

What did we do? After we processed our frustration, we prayed. After all, isn't God our supply? Although He uses man, we can't trust in man. We prayed and asked Jesus to provide the camera one way or another. I knew this was something in His will for our church. It would help us reach way more people. After all, isn't that what we're supposed to be doing?

Our church was located directly off of a major freeway, not very far from the interstate. Because of our location, we'd get many solicitations for money or emergency help. Sometimes these requests would be legit needs. Other times, they'd be scam artists who were "working the system", getting funding from every church in our area. Many times, people would just burst into my office without warning. One moment I'd be studying, and the next minute I'd be wondering if I was about to get robbed by gunpoint!

This became alarming. Because of obvious security reasons, we began to keep the office complex locked. One afternoon, my youth pastor and I were in the fellowship hall doing a few things. Suddenly, I heard a knock at the door. It startled me.

Looking out, I saw a man who was greasy from head to toe. He was in an old beat up work truck. I'd been here before, so I thought.

I have to admit that my first impression was, "Oh no, not again." While I'll take responsibility for my attitude, I must say that dealing with that type of situation multiple times a week becomes taxing. It's easy to grow cynical and cold when you've seen every scam in town. I've been hustled, hookwinked, and cheated out of my last $20 more times than I'd like to admit. I looked at Matt and said, "Your turn." He went down the hall and met with the gentleman. After a few moments of speaking, he motioned for me to come over. This guy had requested to speak to me. I had no idea what would transpire next.

He looked at me and said, "You don't know me, and I don't know you. My wife and I live in the next town over. As I was driving by, the Holy Spirit told me to pull in here and to give this to you." I was wide-eyed and spellbound. I had no idea what to say. Truthfully, I felt like a piece of garbage. He reached into his shirt, pulled out an envelope, and said, "God told me to tell you to do what's in your heart." He then grabbed my hand and asked if he could pray with me. He boldly prayed in the name of Jesus, asking Him to bless our ministry. He then jumped back in the truck and disappeared.

I dashed into my office to open the envelope, and to my surprise, it was five crisp $100 bills! I laughed, cried, and shouted all at the same time! I may have even called those board members and said, "I told you so!" Seeing the error of their decision and failure to trust my lead, many of those men repented and asked me to forgive them.

We got our camera, started a media ministry, and that's all she wrote. This miracle may seem small and insignificant to you, but it certainly wasn't to us. In that season of life, $500 might as well have been $50,000. I needed it, I didn't have it, and I had no idea how I would get it. Through rejection and desperation, God taught me how to use my faith to believe Him for my needs.

I learned several lessons through this mysterious stranger who showed up one rainy afternoon. First of all, God's will is always God's bill. If He guides, He provides. It's not my job to pay for it. It's my job to believe for it. Second, He can use anyone He desires. Last but not least, He taught me not to judge a book by it's cover. As it turns out, he was a businessman. He ended up becoming a great friend to our family.

What's the moral of this story? Never give up on God. If He puts something in your heart, believe Him for it! Prayer makes the impossible possible!

"If you seek nothing but the will of God, He will always put you in the right place at the right time."

-Smith Wigglesworth

CHAPTER SEVEN
"The Drunk Man"

Most of my ministry to the Masai has been exploratory missions and church planting. Aside from that, I love to do crusade ministry. These are typically big outdoor meetings where you put up a stage, have some music, and draw a large crowd. Usually, you'd preach the Gospel and give an altar call, which results in people coming to Christ. When done with strategy and planning, the harvest can be massive.

On this particular trip, several of my best friends accompanied us. Joining us was Pastor Eliot Morgan, Evangelist Grady Watson, and a few other lay people from our churches. We put together two locations and decided to have a Gospel crusade that focused on healing and miracles. After all, the late T.L Osborn said, "Healing is the dinner bell of the Gospel!" In other words, nothing gets people's attention like miracles.

We were in the city center of Narok, a Kenyan city with a large population. We decided to set up our equipment in one of the roughest parts of town. Drug addicts, alcoholics, and homeless people were the main constituency in this neighborhood. We were right where we needed to be. After all, Jesus told us that the Kingdom belongs to the outcast. Along the main street were several shops and bars. People would go and get wasted during the daytime hours, doing anything they could to escape reality. While I don't advocate the use of drugs and alcohol, I can definitely see why people would want to mask their pain and suffering. Poverty causes people to lose hope.

Every day, our team and a group of local Bible school students went out and invited the masses to come. We'd spend about four hours canvassing communities, looking for people to share Jesus with. We'd point them to the city center and tell them about the crusade, pleading with them to bring their friends and relatives. One thing we learned very quickly — Time doesn't matter much to Kenyans! You might say that the meeting will start at 4 pm, but people may not get there until 7 pm! Usually, the sound of music blaring from the busted loud speaker is enough to get people to start moving your direction. Then, one by one, the crowd begins to form.

On this particular night, I'd been tasked to bring the message. Throughout the day, I'd been praying and asking the Holy Spirit what He wanted me to share. I didn't want to pull out my best sermon. These people needed a word from God Himself. Finally, I was led to the Gospel of John. Instantly, I knew I was supposed to preach about the woman at the well. She'd been going from relationship to relationship looking for satisfaction, but it only left her empty inside. Jesus used the illustration of water to show her that only He could satisfy her longing soul. She didn't need Jacob's well: She needed Living Water! I began to think and quietly pray to myself as we walked up and down the dusty roads.

Clean water is very scarce in that part of the world. For many, drinking unclean water can cause serious illness. I found a large bucket and began a search to find drinkable water. We stumbled upon the home of a lady who graciously allowed us to fill our bucket from her water tank. You see, I needed something to get the people's attention. I was going to preach a message called "Give Me a Drink." I planned to conclude this sermon by asking people to come to Christ and allow Him to quench their thirst. I got a little crazy during the delivery of this message. About halfway through, to make a point, I began to reach my hand into the bucket and throw water out onto the crowd. I have to admit to you that I wasn't sure how well that would go over. I do believe it made the point.

I felt so strong that it was time for me to close the message, so I began to shift gears. What happened next had never happened to me before. It's challenging to even describe the event in words. However, I will do my very best. As I was preaching, I kept feeling drawn towards the left side of the stage. I noticed that there was a bar there, and as we were preaching, people were going in and out of it unaffected by our presentation.

Because of the strength of our sound system, I knew these people could hear us anyways. Then, it happened.

As I was beginning to do the altar call, I had what was almost like an out-of-body experience. Now, before you write me off, let me explain: It was as if I was standing outside of my body looking down at myself. I could see the people, I could see my actions, and I could hear my words. It was like a preview of the future. Whether you'd call it a vision, I don't know. I've since learned that for me, it's how God shows me something in the future.

Now, before you say I'm crazy, just hear me out: Every time I've acted on or repeated what I've seen in a revelation like this, it's happened just as I saw it. I now have come to understand that this is a manifestation of the word of wisdom and word of knowledge, both of which Paul referenced in 1 Corinthians 11. They are supernatural gifts whereby the Holy Spirit shows or imparts to you insight or information you would never know in the natural.

As I watched, I saw myself point to the bar and say, "You men in the bar -- Listen to me. There's a man in there tonight. When you were a young boy, God called you to preach the Gospel. You've turned your back on Jesus. Today, it's time to come home to Him. Come, come right now and give your life to Jesus before it's too late. He's calling you back tonight." Before I realized it, I repeated what I saw. Had I hesitated or thought about it first, I likely wouldn't have done it. Talk about stepping out in faith! The Holy Spirit had even given me the age of the man.

As we continued to compel the lost to come forward, the crowd burst out in applause. A drunk man wearing a blue shirt came walking out of the bar. He made his way to the front and knelt down in the dirt. He was weeping. Seven other men from the bar followed his example. This was the man! He came back home to Jesus that night!

Upon our team interviewing him, he was the exact age that the Holy Spirit had shown me. He was called to preach as a young child. He had grown up in the church. However, he'd been hurt by Christians. Some dishonest financial dealings had left him in ruins. Because he was a Christian and a salesman, people took advantage of his generosity. Many cheated him. It caused him to lose faith in himself, in the church, and ultimately in Jesus. He decided that on this day, he would meet some friends and get drunk with cheap liquor. Life was too much to handle anymore. It was his first time to ever visit a bar!

In his own words, he said, "When he heard a white man describing a backslidden man in a bar, I knew it must be God. He told me my story. I have come to give my life back to Christ." He showed up drunk, but he left sober! He came weeping, but left speaking with tongues! Not only was he forgiven, but he rediscovered his purpose! God gave us many more miracles and salvations that evening, but this one takes the cake!

"If you have worry, you don't have faith. If you have faith, you don't have worry."

- Jack Coe

CHAPTER EIGHT

"He Melted Like Wax"

I've seen a lot of crazy things, but I've never seen anything quite like this. As usual, we took a team out into the deep bush to do exploratory missions. We had gone into a remote area full of rocks, mountains, and trees. We had large off-road vehicles and a truck full of supplies. We heard there were unreached people on the other side of this mountain. Getting there would be difficult, but a soul is worth the risk!

Several of my friends accompanied us on this trip. One of them was "Bubba" Johns. Bubba is not his real name, but since I value my life (and our friendship), I'll leave it at that! First of all, let me say this: If you were to look at Bubba and judge a book by its cover, you would never peg him as being a preacher. He looks like he belongs in the outback of Australia. He's an outdoorsman at heart, trained in survival, and happens

63

to dress the part rather well. In the bush, you'd likely find him with cargo pants, a breathable shirt, a brimmed hat, and a machete at his side. Top this off with a long beard, and he looks like one bad dude! Crocodile Dundee, here we come!

Make no mistake about it though: Even though Bubba was an ex-Marine, he had a heart as big as Texas. He and his wife serve as Chi Alpha directors in Louisiana. Chi Alpha is the college campus ministry of the Assemblies of God. We had been on several trips together, but this one was far from ordinary.

After we had gotten to the top of this very large mountain, we received permission from the locals to set up our camp on their land. Setting up a base camp involves clearing brush and debris from the ground, putting up tents, establishing a restroom area, and setting up a makeshift kitchen. Then, we establish multiple controlled fires around the parameter. Not only does this provide warmth and light in the cold, dark night, but it also helps to ward off the animals. From this spot, each day we rise, meet with Jesus in prayer, and go out to give people an opportunity to hear about Him.

Day after day, we'd awaken to the African sunrise and the sounds of people stirring. Our nose would be met by the most wonderful aroma of a makeshift bush kitchen. Maurice, our camp cook, makes everything from scratch. Even if you're not a breakfast eater, you don't miss an opportunity to eat his food. After breakfast, we would all gather around for a time of devotion and prayer. A team member is asked the night before to prepare a lesson for the rest of us, and is then given the opportunity to share their heart. Then, we lift our voices to God and ask for His guidance and protection. It's much easier to take the day knowing He has gone before us.

After breakfast, the team would then brush their teeth, use the restroom facilities, and pack up any items that they'd wish to take with them for the day. Often we'd travel far from the base camp, which meant we wouldn't return until late in the evening. Water, snacks, and other essentials in our bags were a good way to hold off hunger until our return.

On this particular day, the team had departed back to their tents to get ready to depart. To our surprise, a very tall Masai, man, likely in his late 20's, began to approach our camp. As he got closer, we realized he was carrying a small child. One of our African pastors rushed out to greet him. It turns out; he had journeyed from afar because he had heard there were Christians in the area. Word had gotten out among the established churches that missionaries had come from America to reach the Masai and that Jesus was performing miracles.

When we asked the dear man what he needed prayer for, he mentioned to us that his daughter, whom he was carrying, was in desperate need of a miracle. She was 14 months old and was born partially paralyzed. From the neck down, she couldn't use her entire left side. The arm and leg were both atrophied and lifeless. This condition hindered her ability to crawl, walk, and do the other things normal children her age would do.

We decided to pray. Only a few of us were out of our tents, fully ready and waiting to leave. We laid hands on her, and we began to call on the name of Jesus. Our faith and expectation was high. After all, miracles in the bush are common. After moments of prayer, nothing physically changed. Outwardly, I felt defeated and embarrassed. This father came expecting a miracle. Perhaps I shouldn't have felt this way. I'm not the Healer and I possess no power of my own. Yet, I felt his pain. He wanted his child well, and he had traveled far, believing for Jesus to do something. After we stopped praying, we continued to gather our belongings as we prepared for our ministry.

All of a sudden, Bubba unzips his tent, toothbrush in his mouth, and asks, "What's all the racket? What's going on?" We shared details with him and how we'd been asked to pray. He responded, "Well, did she get healed?" I explained that while we prayed and believed God, nothing changed externally. I could tell he didn't like that answer, so I told him, "Well, she's still here if you'd like to pray again." That's all he needed to hear.

Bubba went and introduced himself to the father, and we began to pray a second time. As we began to call out to Jesus, we could feel God's presence. Bubba had compassion, and compassion always moves the heart of God. As I've said before, Masai men can appear cold or emotionless. This is just a facade. It's due to their training as warriors and hunters. As we prayed, this dad seemed to stand there unmoved. The little girl watched us intently. As we prayed, I could sense the Spirit of God tell me, "Put your index finger under her thumb."

That's when the miracle happened! As I took my finger and placed it in the palm of the her hand, she grabbed it. She took my hand and pulled it up over her head. Though trained not to show emotion, this dad lost it. He began to weep as his body fell to the ground, overwhelmed by God's love and mercy. He melted like wax.

A testimony came to us several days later that she had started crawling and learning to walk! There's certainly a lesson to be learned here. First of all, don't be moved by what you see. Next, we see the power of compassion. It's the key to the healing anointing. Finally, we must keep contending! A blessing comes when we persist in faith.

"We cannot exercise our faith beyond what we believe to be possible."

- John G. Lake

CHAPTER NINE

"God and a Grocery List"

Anyone who thinks that people go into the ministry for an easy income is sadly misinformed. While the world sees the flashy televangelists with their jet planes and mailing lists, I can assure you that most ministers are grossly underpaid. The fact is, ministry is way more than just preaching.

Not only is there the time and preparation to produce weekly sermons, but when you add in the administrative tasks, crisis counseling, and community events, the hours can become long and taxing. To be honest, if most church boards added up the hours their pastor actually worked and calculated their "hourly" rate of pay, they'd be embarrassed. The ministry is 24/7, 365 days a year. The truth is, most ministers follow the call because they have a strong desire to follow Christ and to reach the lost., not for money.

When Blonnie and I made the jump to our first full-time ministry position, we weren't concerned about the pay. We were young, without children, and were ready to tackle an adventure together. I walked away from a job that had good pay, an amazing retirement, and a generous vacation policy. For a guy my age with no college degree, it was the best thing available to me. Blonnie had worked her way through cosmetology school, landing herself with a good clientele and a steady income. She hustled hard to work herself into a management position in a corporate salon.

As hard as it was, we left it all behind. Every ounce of security was now in the rear view mirror of our Uhaul truck. We made our way from the most southern part of Arkansas to the midwest. Oklahoma was now our home. My job was to start a youth ministry.

This particular church had a vibrant history in the community. At one time, it was the largest church in town. By the time we arrived on staff, the church had fought through both moral failure and decline. They weren't thriving -- They were merely existing. The salary they offered us was nill in comparision to the compensation we left behind. We knew it would be hard, but we accepted anyhow. After all, it will cost you way more than money to be out of the will of God. We tithed, gave to missionaries, and tried our very best to steward what was entrusted to us.

In general, relocating is hard. With it comes house hunting, changing banks, the opening of new accounts, and making new friends. Just getting there -- That's what I hate. I'm convinced that moving trucks and cross country drives are of the devil himself! At this point, if God ever tells me to move again, I'm selling everything and starting fresh!

Despite all of the hardships of starting over, we were excited. We didn't have a lot, but we had each other. While that sounds corny to some, I mean it. My bride is my best friend. Like a good husband, my desire was to provide for her. Though children weren't yet in the picture, I still strived to make sure she had what she needed to feel secure. In the adjustment period of this move, there were times our faith was stretched -- and so were our finances.

I was mentored by some of the best there is in ministry. I was taught that when you have a need, you take it to the Lord in prayer. I was advised never to be what we call a "poor mouth" preacher. What is a poor mouth preacher? "Poor mouthing" is the art of dropping hints around people in hopes that they will feel sorry for you and meet your need. You dont have to be a minister to use this method. I know plenty of people who are professionals! If you always rely on natural, fleshly solutions to meet your needs, you'll never learn to trust God to the fullest.

Our very first holiday season in Oklahoma was tight. We had moved in October, and the trips back to visit family for Thanksgiving and Christmas had placed a significant burden on our budget. It wasn't just red: It was crimson. "Past due" was my middle name. I was both embarrassed and ashamed.

The cabinets were bare. We needed groceries in a bad kind of way. We weren't to the point of heading to the local soup kitchen just yet, but we were down to the last can of green beans.

Payday was just on the coming Friday, but it seemed like an eternity away. I can remember Blonnie saying how she wished we could run to the store and get some things to hold us over. You know -- roast, cubed steak, chicken, and some ground beef. I don't know where this came from other than the Holy Spirit, but I encouraged her to make a grocery list. This may sound crazy if you don't have any money, but faith starts stepping even when you can't see the whole staircase. After all, Habakkuk 2:2 says, "Write the vision and make it plain…"

She got busy writing. When she would get alone, she'd take the list to God in prayer. Through seasons like this, here's what I've learned: Our faith isn't developed when we're on the mountain tops of life. No! Faith is produced in the valley of the shadow of death! Although not comfortable to our flesh, situations like these cause spiritual growth.

The day after our grocery list was made, there was a knock on our front door. It was early on a Saturday, so we thought it might have been a Mormon or a Jehovah's Witness. After all, they would stop by every once in a while with the hope to make a convert out of me. Boy, was I wrong. It was Mrs. Lynda Quattlebaum. She was a member of our church and had been an enormous encouragement to my family. She apologized for coming by so early, but said she felt impressed of the Holy

Spirit to be a blessing to our family. Although we looked a mess, we invited her inside.

While she was doing her morning shopping, the Holy Spirit nudged her to be a blessing to their new youth pastors. She said, "I didn't really know what kind of stuff you guys like, so I hope this is ok." She handed us several grocery bags filled with freshly wrapped meat from the butcher shop. I must admit that when she left, it felt a little bit like Christmas morning. We couldn't wait to see what was under all of that wrapping. Much to our surprise, every item on our list was in that bag! All we could do was cry. Once again, we were amazed at His goodness, kindness, and mercy toward His servants.

Now, God has blessed us to be in a much different season of life. He's given us way more than we ever deserve. Every so often, when I feel a nudge to give to the poor, buy someone's groceries, or help a family at Christmas, I'm reminded of how God helped us. I remember what it felt like to feel hopeless, alone, and like a failure.

What I learned from this situation is simple, but has stuck with me throughout the years. That simple truth is this: Always be obedient. You never know when God will use you to be the answer to someone else's prayer.

"Faith is all about believing. You don't know how it will happen, but you know it will."

- Author Unknown

CHAPTER TEN
"Supernatural Surgery"

The account I'm about to share is closer to home than I'd like to admit. I've seen a lot of miracles, but this time, I'd be needing one. I've discovered that being used for God and by God doesn't exempt you from trouble. In fact, I believe that the call of God makes us a greater target for adversity.

For those who've experienced appendicitis or kidney stones, the pain is no laughing matter. "Debilitating" is a word commonly associated with that kind of ailment. I was 32 years old and pastoring in central Louisiana when I was struck with unusual pain. That weekend was filled with grading tests at our state ministry school.

All of a sudden, intense pain radiated down into my groin area. It sent me into a fetal position. The pain was unbearable.

I'd never felt anything like this. On a scale of 1 - 10, it was a 20! I went home and endeavored to sleep this off. Like most men, I avoid the doctor's office like the plague. As a minister of the Gospel, I wholeheartedly believe that Jesus is our Healer. While I don't discourage people from using medicine, I do challenge them to pray first. If we never exercise our faith, how can we believe for a miracle? If you still need a physician or medicine after prayer, do what you need to achieve relief. There's no shame in that whatsoever. Either way, healing is always the will of God. I prayed, took some over the counter medicine, and drifted off to sleep.

The aching throb woke me up in the middle of the night. It was then that I finally decided to go to the hospital. Thankfully, the closest emergency room was less that two miles away.

After all of the scans, x-rays, lab work, and ultrasounds, the ER doctor told me that he detected a mass on my left kidney. Due to the scope of his field, he was hesitant to tell me anything specific, but instead stressed that I see a urologist as quickly as possible.

I made an appointment for the first thing on Monday morning. My time slot was at 10:30 am., but I arrived two hours early. Noticing the distressed look on my face, they had mercy on me and let me go back early. After Dr. Bass looked at my diagnostics, he suggested a more thorough scan using a special contrast. Injected intraveneously, a special dye would flow throughout the circulatory system. Once it reached the kidneys, it would show the detail of any abnormality they would find. He was so concerned about my situation that he scheduled it for the same day. A technician put his hand on my shoulder and said, "Come with me." I walked down the cold hall of the hospital, praying that perhaps the previous test was a fluke. Maybe the pain I had experienced was some freak thing.

I was positioned on the examining table. It was cold. The radiologist placed the I.V. in my hand, and with a few clicks of a button, the dye rushed through my veins. Within 30 seconds, a metallic taste hit the back of my throat. They assured me that this was normal. Then, the scan began.

The technician told me that the doctor would come in, read it, and tell me what was going on. It didn't exactly turn out that way. Laying on the table, I saw him come in and speak with the technician. It was behind a window, so I couldn't hear their conversation. However, I saw the expression on his face. He abruptly turned and walked out of the room -- and never came back. I wanted answers, and I wanted them right now.! The man assisting with my procedure assured me that the doctor would be calling first thing in the morning. I left with more questions than I did answers.

The next day, the doctor called and told us to come in. Upon signing in, they called me back immediately. Before exchanging a greeting or any pleasantries, I asked him, "What in the world is going on?" He explained that they had discovered a complex renal cyst deep within my left kidney. It was the size of a grapefruit. Under normal circumstances, this type of cyst could be biopsied. If needed, they can be surgically removed. Not this one though. This was in an unreachable place. Besides that, the new scan revealed more information.

Unlike a normal renal cyst, this one had a complex blood supply. According to all the medical data and research, this indicated that the cyst was cancerous and nothing to play around with. He admitted to me that the reason he didn't come back into the room that day was because he had to talk himself out of doing emergency surgery on the spot! He wanted to remove my kidney.

Because of my age, he wanted to consult with the whole urology team at the hospital before making such a life changing decision. After discussing their findings, they determined the best course of action was to watch it for four months to see if there was any growth. Then, based on current scans, they would decide the best course of treatment. That wasn't exactly what I wanted to hear. I had a decision to make: I could accept this diagnosis as my destiny, or I could choose to live by the faith that I preached to others. I began a season of intense fasting and prayer. I cranked up my ministering to the sick. I'm a firm believer that when you are standing in faith for your own needs, one of the best things you can do is get your mind on others.

On March 20, our church hosted a women's conference. To give you the timeline, this was about two months and a few days into my "waiting period." As the pastor, I was there to make sure everything ran smoothly. I opened the building, turned on the sound system, and assisted some volunteers who were setting up product tables for our guest.

This conference was geared for women, not for a guy like me! I stayed as far out of sight as possible! God has a sense of humor, doesn't He? During the service, the conference speaker was preaching about the healing power of God. Though he was emphasizing the healing of the mind and emotions, he asked everyone who needed a touch from God to come forward. I was hanging on to every word. I felt a nudge to go up and get prayer, but my pride was screaming, "You're not a lady!" I went anyway.

I told him exactly what I needed and where the pain was located. He laid his hands on it, and he and I agreed in faith. We stood on Mark 11:23-25 and "spoke to the mountain" that was lodged inside my kidney. I felt something physically shift in my body. When God touches you, you just know it.

I told everybody from that point, "I know that I'm healed." Because this event and the follow-up appointment had some time between them, the devil would come and try to bring doubt into my heart. I had to continually stand on God's Word, rebuke Satan, and tell him to leave me alone.

On Tuesday, May 5, I went back in for my follow-up appointment and CT scan. Once again, the doctor didn't give me the results immediately. The devil tried to say, "Here you go again." I waited for days on end for a phone call, but it never came. I couldn't take the anticipation any longer.

I called the office on Friday, May 8, and kindly demanded an answer. The nurse insisted that they still needed me to come in to the office, but she had permission to share some good news: She told me the mass in my kidney was completely gone! It was undetectable. Only a tiny scar remained where it used to be. In her own words, "Only a small scar remains. It looks as if someone already cut it out." Back at that women's conference in March, the Lord performed supernatural surgery. If faith can move a mountain, a mass is no problem!

"Often times we say, 'I know God can, but…'. Let your faith be bigger than your 'but!'"
- Author Unknown

CHAPTER ELEVEN
"My Jonah Season"

A s I shared in a previous chapter, I experienced the call of God at the young age of fourteen. My school friends made fun of me. I was called a "Bible thumper," "holy roller," and a "Jesus freak." I took my Bible to class, tried my best to live a holy life, and with compassion, I shared my faith with others. Many of those same classmates who bullied me have since bought my books, listened to my sermons, and have contacted me to pray for their families!

As much as I'd like to tell you that I stayed on the straight and narrow, I can't. I had a season that was nothing short of rebellion. I didn't fall away from God -- I ran away from Him. That's why I refer to this as my "Jonah Season." Jonah was called to save Nineveh, but in turn, he ran as far away in the as he could. His willful disobedience caused unrest not only in his own life, but in the life of others. He ended up being thrown off of a ship and being swallowed by a giant fish. It sounds crazy, but for three days and nights, God preserved him. Jonah cried out to the Lord from the belly of the fish, and God heard him. He finally surrendered. Jonah was ejected from the belly of the fish back onto dry ground. What happened next is beautiful.

Jonah 3:1-2 says, "Now the word of the Lord came unto Jonah a second time….." To me, this is perhaps one of the most redemptive verses in the entirety of the Bible. Its open display of mercy and grace shows us that even when we get off track, He still has a plan for us. His gifts and callings are irrevocable! Allow me to continue.

By the age of 14, I already had a beautiful testimony. I knew God was real, I knew His call over my life was valid, and I knew that I would spend the rest of my life preaching His Word. I had no plan b. This was it.

The ministry I was connected to was vibrant and alive. Those people greatly loved Jesus, their community, and young people like me. I felt loved, accepted, and connected to the leadership. They did their very best to mold me into a disciple of Christ. That said, many of the younger leaders were controlling.

It wasn't uncommon for them to make you tell them what you'd been watching, who you were attracted to, and what you did with your free time. Hear me out on this one: There's a fine like between accountability and control. One is entered into freely while the other is exerted by force. At the time, I didn't realize this type of behavior was sowing seeds of rebellion into my heart. I was slowly beginning to pull away from God, and they didn't even see it. I was experimenting with all types of substances and sin. I felt terrible about it, but I would keep doing it anyway. I was dangling over the edge of a cliff, and no one seemed to care.

When I was 16, I met a gorgeous young lady while working in my dad's store. I jokingly say "young", but she was a few years older than me. I instantly fell in love with her. She was attractive to my eyes, but the more I got to know her, the beauty of her soul overshadowed her physical features. Blonnie Holland was her name.

While she didn't come from a Christian home, her parents had strong moral values. They believed that family was a priority, that love was unconditional, and that hard work was noble. They were small business owners who had been faithfully married to each other for decades.

In high school, Blonnie was such a free-spirited soul. Her adventurous nature attracted the same type of friends. To some, she was considered, "the life of the party." To my church leaders and friends, she was anything but girlfriend material. Although I witnessed to her and invited her to church, they told me she wasn't good enough. To be very direct, I was told, "If you don't leave that girl alone, you're going to bust Hell wide open." I was dangling over the edge spiritually, but that pushed me straight over.

I was tired of judgemental religious people. I ran swiftly into a life of sin, not taking regard for any of the consequences to follow. Smoking, cursing, and sexual immorality became my regular routine. I could care less if I ever stepped back in a church! I was having the best time of my life -- or so I thought.

We'd been dating for a solid year when I realized that I wanted to spend the rest of my life with her. In July of 2000, I popped the question. I'm so grateful she said yes! Shortly after graduation, we married. I found a great paying job with benefits and retirement. With no college education, it was definitely a score.

Though I was married and working, I was still trying to go to the parties all night. I was in a successful band. Our calendar was full of weekend events ranging from bars, private parties, and festivals. I'd party all night and work the day shift with no sleep, or I'd hang out all day and work the graveyard shift like a zombie. It wasn't a glamorous way to live.

One evening, we were invited to play a party at a private residence. The day was spent with rehearsals and setting up sound equipment. It was certainly fun, but I had to report to work at 11 pm. That 11 pm - 7 am graveyard shift was brutal! At 10:45 pm, I rushed quickly across town to avoid being late for work. I barely made it. I have no idea how I completed my shift that night. It was only by God's grace.

As shift change approached, a wave of drowsiness hit me that I just couldn't shake. For the first time, I was afraid I might not be able to make it home. The thought of falling asleep at the wheel was terrifying. Someone at work had a bottle of pills they had purchased at the truck stop and offered to let me have some. These pills were a combination of ephedrine and caffeine, both of which can be deadly in excess. Having never taken them before, I was skeptical. Hesitant or not, I was also desperate. I proceeded anyway.

As the time to go home got closer, I felt anything but "stimulated." Were these pills going to wake me up, or are were they some fake placebo? Perhaps I didn't take enough. I ended up taking half a bottle! If I'd ever had a lapse of judgment, it was then. To top it off, I drank 40 ounces of cold coffee on an empty stomach. As crazy as it sounds, I still wasn't feeling it -- then I got in my car.

About halfway home, I began to feel strange. I'm not sure what a heart attack feels like, but I thought I had one! All of a sudden, massive amounts of pressure was on my chest. I was rushed to the ER and given medication to slow my heart rate and calm my anxiety. I thought I was going to die that morning.

This event scared me so much that it threw me into a series of debilitating panic attacks. This hellacious torment lasted for five solid months. From May until September, my days were filled with anxiety, chest pain, and nausea. I would dry heave a minimum of five times per day. I was malnourished. I couldn't keep food down, nor could I hold a job. It was definitely a strain on our new marriage. We sought medical help. The doctors tried medication after medication with no success. The truth is, I didn't need medicine: I needed repentance!

On September 11, 2001, our nation experienced one of it's greatest tragedies -- Islamic terrorism on American soil. Several Muslim radicals boarded commercial flights with one purpose: to hit America where it hurts -- Our economy. They hijacked the planes, and two of them struck the Twin Towers, killing many innocent lives in the process.

We were still lying in bed when the phone rang. It was Tim, the lead singer of my band. He told me to turn on the television. He was frantic. As soon we did, we witnessed the second plane exploding into the second tower. It didn't seem real. America was under attack.

Blonnie was frightened. She cried out, "If I die, I don't know where I'll spend eternity. I don't have a relationship with God!" I'd never heard her speak this way. We never talked about Jesus in our home. We were living like sinners and enjoying every minute of it. I was so shocked that I almost asked her to repeat herself! She turned to me and said, "When I first met you, you told me you were going to be a preacher. I didn't mean to get you off track. I need to get right with God!"

I was as far away from God in that moment as a person could be. I couldn't recall a single Scripture to memory. I hadn't truly prayed in years. However, her words pierced my soul. She asked me to pray with her. I struggled through it, but I did.

That morning, I prayed and asked Jesus to forgive me, to help me get back on track, and to restore me. Such a peace filled my heart. All of the weight and pressure lifted. I felt "alive" again. I grabbed her hands, and we prayed together.

With a rusty prayer, I led her to Christ. I was backslidden one moment and a soul winner the next.

I was tired of running from God. Like Jonah, today was the day to surrender. Not only was my spirit and soul restored, but so was my body. The five month battle was over. My sickness left that day and never came back! A season of torment was gone in an instant.

Several weeks after coming home to Christ, the Holy Spirit began to help me put my life back together. In prayer, He told me, "I'm going to give you back what the enemy has stolen." To be honest, he had stolen a lot! He robbed me of my peace, my health, my productivity, and my happiness.

I felt impressed by God to call my previous employer and ask for my job back. I had gotten fired for missing too much work (due to sickness), so I knew that God would have to work a miracle. Not only did they give me my job back, but they stuck me in a different department with better pay!

For the first time as a couple, we started going to church together. Even though I recommitted my life to Christ, the ministry was nowhere in my plans. I figured that ship had sailed a long time ago. After all, I was content with where I was. Though we were attending church and growing spiritually, we both held on to things that Jesus needed us to let go of.

Particularly, I was still playing gigs with my band. For years, these guys were my closest friends. I didn't want to abandon them and quit. Playing music isn't inherently wicked, but entertaining people in clubs, bars, and parties were now contradictory to my testimony. Aside from that, the type of music we were playing was anything but godly. I knew I needed to close this chapter in my life. It would be the last key to fully surrendering my heart to Him.

One month after our household transformation, my band was asked to host a benefit for the Red Cross. The proceeds would go to help clean up the mess made at Ground Zero on 9/11. Because this was for a "good cause", I justified doing it. After all, God likes charity, right?

The night was going great. People from all over our region came to support us. As we went up to do our set, I heard a voice say, "What are you doing here?" I stopped. I immediately recognized His voice. It was the same voice I heard at 14 years old. At that moment, it was game over. I knew this was it. To keep my word, I went ahead and played the show. The next day, I quit the band. They were very upset with me. Regardless, I had to do what I had to do. I walked away and never looked back!

That night in a bar, Jesus called me a second time. He didn't have to. He could've easily used someone else. Yet, He saw in me what I couldn't see in myself! Like Jonah, the word of the Lord came to me a second time. I'm so grateful for His mercy and grace!

"Be obedient. You may be God's answer to another person's prayer."

- Shane Warren

CHAPTER TWELVE
"Jesus Loves Lesbians"

O ften on this journey called life, we encounter people who leave a lasting impression upon our souls. I'm deeply convinced that as we follow the leadership of the Holy Spirit, He places the right people in our lives exactly when we need them. I call these divinely orchestrated relationships "Kingdom Connections."

While I was pastoring in Monticello, Arkansas, a close friend shared with me that revival had broken out in a women's correctional facility. To be clear, when I mention the word "revival", I'm not referencing one of those planned three-day events geared to make people excited about Jesus. This was the real deal. God was pouring out His Spirit. The ladies may have been bound, but His mercy and grace weren't.

Through mutual friends, God connected us with Aly Atwood, the chaplain of Louisiana Transitional Center for Women. Her facility was located in Tallulah, Louisiana -- a small town with nothing but a Popeye's Chicken! Quietly tucked away in the middle of nowhere, Jesus was changing lives. Under her leadership, it grew from a small Bible study to over 400 women nightly! What was once a dungeon of shame quickly transformed into a house of hope! With her invitation, we joined her efforts and put together a team.

I reached out to Taylor Shoats and asked her to lead worship for us. She had gone to Kenya with me many times and had become like my little sister. Her spirit was as pure as anyone I had ever worked with. Not only did she have an amazing voice, but she had a true prophetic gift upon her life. I knew I could trust her heart to minister to these hurting ladies.

Then, I reached out to Scotty Sneed, a beloved brother who lived in the same town as me. He was a kindred spirit. Scotty genuinely had compassion for the sick and hurting. It was because of this that he saw many people saved and healed by the power of God! He was a big help in ministering to them one on one.

I could write a whole separate book just on the miracles and salvations that occurred behind those prison doors! Hundreds of women came to faith in Christ, were baptized in the Holy Spirit, and were healed of diseases. I've lost track of the number of women that told us that they had planned to kill themselves, but Jesus restored their hope!

One particular night, I told Taylor that I felt like Jesus wanted to set people free from sexual perversion. In the prison system, people often turn to homosexuality to meet their penned up desires. For others, they use it as a way to establish dominance in the cell blocks. Regardless of the reason, we believe homosexuality is sinful and needs deliverance.

As Taylor was singing during the altar call, I proclaimed, "Jesus wants to set lesbians free tonight!" To my surprise, 24 women ran to the front weeping! I took a moment to share God's heart with them concerning their identity and His will for their lives. One by one, they repented, renounced that lifestyle, and gave their lives to Jesus Christ. Many of them we glorious baptized in the Spirit, speaking in a language they had never learned!

No matter what sin a person may be bound with, the power of God can set them free. No matter how dirty they are, the blood of Christ can wash them clean. Jesus loves lesbians, and He loves you too!

"When you feed your faith, you starve your doubts."

- Lester Sumrall

CHAPTER THIRTEEN

"Just a Whisper"

I f there's one thing for sure, it's this: The western world is blessed when it comes to modern medicine. You and I think nothing of treating minor ailments. It's not something we usually even think about.

Have a stomach ache? Grab some pink stuff. Head pounding? Grab some Advil. While I appreciate the modern advances we have in medicine, I certainly believe they have set us back in regularly seeing healing miracles. Why? We don't have to rely on God as much.

Let's be honest here. I also find myself guilty at times. How often have we run to a pill before we've even tried prayer? To see the supernatural, we must give God an opportunity.

In third world nations, this is not the case. Not only is preaching the Gospel a catalyst for the supernatural, but so is desperation. When you don't have anything to fall back on, that's when your need for Jesus is realized the most. This is the sole reason why you notice people's prayer life ramp up when tragedy strikes.

In remote areas of Kenya, certain diseases seem to be prevalent. First, we see HIV and AIDS. This is due to many unsanitary actions such as unsafe sex practices, female sexual mutilation, and unclean needles. Blindness is also prevalent among the elderly. Some of this is systemic, while other is caused by viral and bacterial diseases that form in the eyes due to unclean living conditions. This list isn't exhaustive, but one of the saddest is that of malaria.

According to the CDC, there are approximately 10,700 deaths due to malaria each year. What is malaria, you might ask? Malaria is a parasitic disease transmitted by mosquitoes. The infection causes intense pain, high fever, and in extreme cases, death. Many children and elderly are lost to this disease each year. That is so tragic. It's unnecessary. Why? It costs about $2 to treat.

There are many options to prevent and treat this illness, but one of them is all too common in America — Doxycycline. This antibiotic is used to treat many woes, but its success in malaria treatment is paramount. What's the issue? As they say in the real estate business, "Location, location, location!" The very place the people live mixed with poverty makes the chance of survival slimmer.

Mikey Cheshier, my best friend, and teammate, walked into a particular bush village to share his testimony. Mikey was burned as a child, and his story captivates the listener. As we approached, we quickly realized that all the men were out working and doing their daily duties. Being a highly patriarchal culture, we usually do our best to minister to the men first. We've found out that if we can get their honor and respect, the rest will follow their lead. However, that opportunity wasn't available for us on this day.

As we exchanged our pleasantries, a small child around three years old was screaming at the top of its lungs. This little boy, according to our translator, was suffering from a terrible case of malaria. We reached down to greet the little fellow, and his head was blistering hot. Without exaggeration, you likely could've cooked an egg on it. It's challenging to share the Gospel while a child is making that kind of commotion. However, it's not always a sermon that a person needs first. In this case, it was a demonstration of compassion.

Moved with pure love, Mikey reached down and placed his hand on the child's forehead. The little guy was spooked. After all, it's very unlikely he'd ever seen a white-skinned person before. Aside from that, a stranger reaching out to touch him was likely unnerving.

When I think of someone laying hands on the sick, my mind races immediately to the classic tent revival preacher, drenched in sweat, a bottle of oil in his hand shouting, "Glory!" However, such was not the case on this day. Mikey laid his hand on the boy and whispered, "Jesus." Immediately, the screaming stopped. Within just a few brief moments, his temperature came back down to normal. Before we left, he was playing with the other children.

After we demonstrated the Gospel to them, their hearts were opened to hearing it. In Scripture, Jesus often healed unbelievers to unlock their hearts and get their attention. It works! Miracles aren't supposed to exalt the preacher: Miracles should point to the Christ inside the believer.

This healing didn't come in a shout -- It came in a whisper. There is great power in the name of Jesus. It calms the raging seas and it heals all manner of disease. Just the whisper of His name is all that's needed.

Epilogue

O ur prayer is that you've been tremendously blessed and inspired by the book. The last thing we want is for you to do walk away, thinking, "How cool!" or, "That's neat." I wanted to inspire you with the enclosed testimonies to let you know that God still does the supernatural with ordinary, everyday people. You don't have to be a missionary or a superstar pastor. All you need to be is a believer!

I want to make something vitally clear: I don't chase miracles. I preach the Gospel in faith, do my best to be compassionate, and Jesus does the rest.

If you have a pure heart and desire to make Jesus famous, there's no limit to what can happen through your yielded life. Sure, you're likely to encounter people who try to put out your fire. Just remember that Jesus is the same yesterday, today, and forever! Stay humble, live holy, and submit your life into His hands.

If you don't know this Jesus we're speaking of, let me invite you to begin a marvelous relationship with Him. In the back of the book is the plan of salvation. Please take the time to read it.

Jesus came, lived, and ultimately died so that you and I, sinners who were separated from God, could have a relationship with Him.

Only through Jesus can we be saved, forgiven, and completely reconciled to God. Without Christ, there's only eternal judgment awaiting all of us. Act now. Today is the day of salvation. He's waiting for you!

In Christ,

Brad Smith

Brad Smith Ministries

"Sometimes, a miracle can manifest
as a good person with
a giving heart."
- Author Unknown

The ABC's of Salvation

ADMIT

Admit to God that you are a sinner. All persons need salvation. Each of us has a problem the Bible calls sin. Sin is a refusal to acknowledge God's authority over our lives. Everyone who does not live a life of perfect obedience to the Lord is guilty of sin.

"For all have sinned and fall short of the glory of God"
(Rom. 3:23).

Since none of us is perfect, all of us are sinners
(Rom. 3:10- 18).

The result of sin is spiritual death (**Rom. 6:23**).

Spiritual death means eternal separation from God. By God's perfect standard, we are guilty of sin and, therefore, subject to the punishment for sin, which is separation from God. Admitting that you are a sinner and separated from God is the first step of repentance, turning from sin and self and turning toward God.

BELIEVE

Believe in Jesus Christ as God's Son and receive Jesus' gift of forgiveness from sin. God loves each of us. God offers us salvation. Although we have done nothing to deserve His love and redemption, God wants to save us. In the death of Jesus on the cross, God provided salvation for all who would repent of their sins and believe in Jesus.

"For God so loved the world that he gave his one and only Son, that whoever believes in him shall not perish but have eternal life"
(John 3:16).

CONFESS

Confess your faith in Jesus Christ as Savior and Lord to others. After you have received Jesus Christ into your life, share your decision with another person. Tell your pastor or a Christian friend about your decision. Following Christ's example, ask for baptism by immersion in your local church as a public expression of your faith.

"If you confess with your mouth, 'Jesus is Lord,' and believe in your heart that God raised him from the dead, you will be saved. For it is with your heart that you believe and is justified, and it is with your mouth that you confess and are saved"
(Rom. 10:9-10).

Available Now On

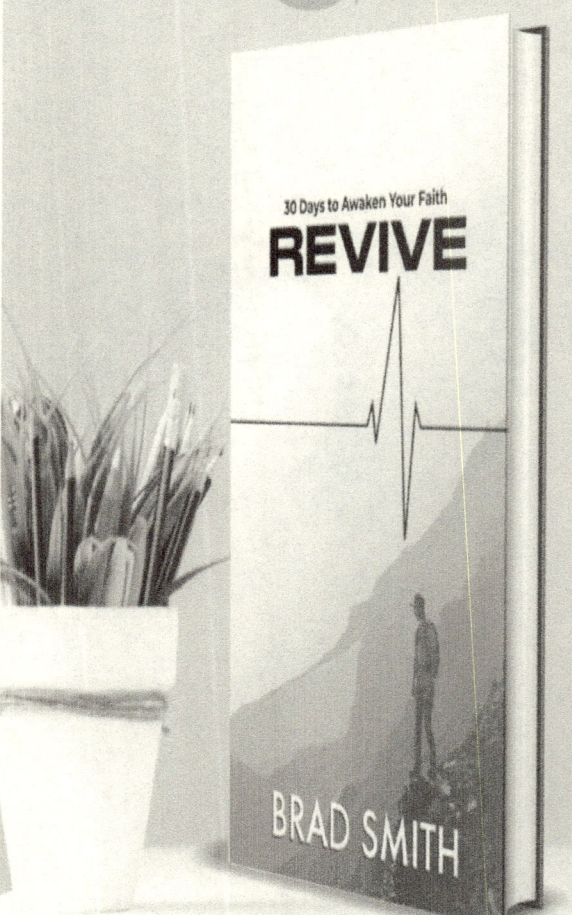

Made in the USA
Monee, IL
13 October 2020